IN A WOMAN'S LIKENESS

Other books by the author:
Accidental Reality (Littlewood, 1989)
Thinking Egg (Littlewood Arc, 1993)

In a WOMAN'S LIKENESS

JACQUELINE BROWN

ARC PUBLICATIONS
1996

Published by Arc Publications
Nanholme Mill, Shaw Wood Road
Todmorden, Lancs. OL14 6DA

Design by Tony Ward
Printed at Arc & Throstle Press
Nanholme Mill, Todmorden, Lancs.

ISBN 1 900072 03 3

Acknowledgements:
Some of these poems have appeared in *Writing Women*, *Other Poetry*, *Staple* and *Iron*.

The Author wishes to thank the Hawthornden Trust for a fellowship which enabled her to write some of the poems included in this collection.

The publishers acknowledge assistance from Yorkshire and Humberside Arts Board.

For my dear friend
Hilda Cotterill

CONTENTS

PART ONE

LEARNING LARK

Learning Lark

I suppose there are some here
the same as everywhere, but,
like an aboriginal with no word
for sailing-ship and therefore
no eyes to see their geometry
slicing his sky, I've never seen one.
But I'm learning lark.

I'm learning woman
from Madame Tippett with her scraps
of hat and scarves of scent, the red
moue of her lips teaching our mouths
to form French vowels like u and eau,
how to reach for r's at the very back
of the throat, learning how to become
a Madame and not a Missis.

I'm learning because I have to.
I can't, won't be a pigeon in a crate
on Baghill Station, named Bluey or Joey,
always homing for food.
I can't, won't be badged with pinny
or headscarf, counting up my life
in hot North Country dinners.

I've been singing it all day in my head
the way you do when a song lodges
in cracks of the brain and repeats,
repeats, teaching you something, encoring
till you get the point, the inflection
spot on, the vowels true, the lesson learned.
I think I've learned lark.

*

Home and my mother's dishevelled
from shopping. Her mouth's a straight line
as she unties the checked square from her hair,
tuts at the time, the muck on my socks,
how money doesn't grow on trees, I know.

I don't have the word for what I feel
so don't have a heart to feel it.
But I'm learning, so . . . . . .

"Have I to sing you the song we learned
in French today?" She's emptying carriers.
I don't wait for assent, just start –
"Alouette, gentille alouette, Alouette,
je te plumerai." The ou and the u
are spot-on, the r is just right.
"What's it mean?" she says.

Mean? All day I've just sung it,
not translated, not needed to translate.
Still there's enough lark for both of us.
"Lark," I say (not seeing the wicker crate
with its lid agape) "Kind lark" (teetering
splayfoot on its rim) "I will pluck you"
(headlong into a slatted space and a lid
slammed shut and strapped tight) Through a gap
I see Mam roll her eyes to the ceiling,
start to assemble spuds for peeling,
her mouth as Yorkshire as a knife.

Where I am now there're just shafts of light,
the rest is all hot, thick, noisy dark.
It won't be easy but I will climb the light.
No Missis will stop me. I will learn lark.

Getting It Wrong

I am the eldest. I arrogate roles round here.
Somewhat afraid to be God, I am Gabriel,
my darkhaired penultimate sister can be Mary.
I do not love her. I give her no words to say,
only a doll with a faulty eye, wrapped tight
in a terry nappy, and instructions to act humble.
My brother is Joseph, first King and would have been
Herod only he jibbed at it. My fairhaired sister
(who I love) is chief shepherd and keeper of the inn.
As each she is reverent, always willing,
her voice modulates sweetly and she never cracks up
laughing as Mary, my flesh-thorn, sometimes does.
The youngest, wide-eyed, with a teatowel transforming
his podgy baby face to boyhood is un- or in- or a-
directable, though he'd die for my archangelic praise.
I love him but it irks when he goes wall-eyed
with bafflement and fear of blame as I spread
my sheeted arms like windmill sails and tell him,
"Look astonished".

We are nearly and then we are there. The evening.
The door flung open. The perfect moment of surprise
and praise. I have only got as far as the tidings
of great joy with the baby looking almost astonished
and fairhaired sister giving it all she's got of awe
and bloody Mary on the bottom step practising simpers
and Joseph hitching up the dressing-gown by its plaited
cord belt – I've only got that far when Dad smiles
a yawn and Mam says "I think it's Frankie Howerd
on the other channel in a minute".

A click and less than a second and that oblong face
with its pout lip and suggestive sideglance
fills the dark room with the voice of God,
each syllable stretched elastic. "Ooo-er," it says.
The overtones and undertones curl me under my sheet
like a slug. But I'm wondering how we'll stage-
manage the crucifixion come Easter even as I retract
to almost nothing.

Ornament

It hung on the living-room wall
above the table where the telly
stood once we got the telly –
the head of a woman in profile,
her Robin Hood hat tipped forward,
her half face as white as sickness,
one blue eye and lips the colour of blood.

For years I watched Coronation Street
and Ready Steady Go sideways-on.
No way I wanted my blue eye to meet hers,
not if I could help it. I knew who she was,
or rather who she had been before they plaster-
casted her death-mask to hang on our wall.

No-one had had to tell me. No-one spoke of her
(just as no-one mentioned my vanished Dad),
but I knew even though the house ballooned
with unasked questions and every cupboard
locked itself on rattling skeleton secrets:
she was my new step-dad's defunct first wife.

Earwigging at the huddle of women talking
in mouse voices, I'd gleaned the odd dropped
word to plait her story. "Muriel" was one,
"Mental Home" two others. They were enough.
I became Jane Eyre and my step-dad Rochester.
His jolly face was just a front that didn't
fool me. It was just because we had no attic
the madwoman loomed from the wall to remind.

Later my mother changed the décor, replaced her
with a gold and silver waterfall in China
with rocks and skinny trees and a very strange
use of perspective. I'd become Emily Brontë
by then and found a rather déclassé Heathcliff
brooding in the town's only coffee-bar, so never
gave Muriel another thought till just the other day

when I saw her again, three or four versions of her
in differing hats among the china at an Antique Fair.
My heart jinked a little even as I giggled
seeing several mad Muriels staring at me there.
Reminding.

Three Wise Monkeys

Almost every house had one then
a present from Filey or Blackpool
or Skegness.   Ours was brass.

It lived on top of the mantelpiece
with the bell and the candlesticks
under the vast circle of sailing-ship,

flanked by the two rectangular plaques
with all the verses of Bless This House
you could read like braille.

A brutish, squat unholy trinity
all its piety translated by Northern spite
into "See all: hear all: say nowt."

It watched us all but me especially,
parting its fifteen fleshless fingers slightly
to squint through, exhale, let the words in,

When fury turned the house dark purple,
when even the cuckoo clock yelled murder
instead of cuckoo, it was there, unperturbed.

Nights when they went out and left me alone
I'd turn its horrid faces to the wall
though the ridged humped back was equally scary,

those nights I'd pit one power against
another, sitting on the couch, whole body tense
with purpose, singing in my devoutest voice
every brass word of Bless This House.

Game

I lie in my thin skin in bed, my brother,
mushroom cool, asleep in the cot beside me.
I must not wake him. He needs to sleep.
He's just a baby. I have been told. She
has told me. Time and time and time again.
The woman in the mirror stretches her eyes.
She strokes the little brush over and over
her lashes. Now she leans into the glass
and paints in her mouth, a red cut in her face.
Now she is brushing her hair that crackles
like a black fire – her hair will not do
as she tells it, no matter how many times.
"Well?" she says to the mirror. "Will I do?"
The mirror won't lie and speak the fairest words
but it is not a telltruth either. Neither am I.
"Beautiful", I lie to her back, as she lies
to me, pretending to love me yet leaving me.
This is one of the rules of the game we play.
Others are: I must not disturb Dad downstairs.
I must be good. I must not wake my little brother.
These are the moves I should make but I cheat
and make others when the woman in the mirror's
not looking. The Queen's rules don't count
once the mirror's gone blank and the door slams.
Then I lean over and shake the baby's cool shoulder.
I watch his eyes open and his mouth go square.
Then he cries.
I can hear the feet on the stairs, the voice
come nearer and nearer, then it's down, down
to the low fire, the big chair, the baby rocked
back to his dreamskin asleep on the couch.
Now I share Daddy's thick skin that grows thicker and
thicker as his voice grows darker, his breath quicker.
Evenings we play by the King's rules that can't be broken.
For the baby's sake, for the glass woman's sake,
I make the moves the game dictates.
Time and time and time again.

Dot

The gap between numbers three and thirteen
was greater than ten, though nobody said so
in so many words – just admonishments not to
accept anything offered when we went to share
our bounty with Dot and the Baxter tribe.
"God knows the poor soul's got little enough
as it is," Mam said as we clacked up the cobbles
bearing our plate of scones or tea cakes,
"And anyway, God knows what you might catch."

It was sheer amazement to stand on the yellow step,
peer into that gloom and see the jam jar tea-cups
and newspaper tablecloth, the rutted rug, the couch
where silent bad-backed Albert lay prone, startling
to hear him hawk and spit on the fire never missing.
I watched the two women ask after each other –
my Mam's blue eyes sympathetic, Dot's broad Yorkshire
vowels answering and muttermutter from Albert's corner.
"No thanks, Auntie Dot," I'd say, and, "Just had one,
thanks, Dot", Mam would say. "Yes. Absolutely sure."

That day when Dot came to ours and we gave her tea
in a proper cup with yellow flowers and a saucer
and spoon, that day I'll remember – how she held
the saucer in the scallop of her hand and picked up
the tiny-handled tea cup with her pinkie stretched out
and slightly curled; how I said aloud, "Oh look at Dot
trying to be posh" and for centuries there was no sound
in the room except our silence. All I could think of
was after. Then the spoon whanged from my Mam's had
to my forehead and my heart clattered as though someone
had dropped a whole canteen of stainless steel cutlery.

The Laugh

Dad, his moods as black as carbon,
laws intransigent – anthracite
burning slow but then heat, beat,
yell, holler – "Steal, would you?"
belt leather on our thinnest skin.
"Lie, would you?" Blue-eyed Dad
boiling up revenge, pouring it out.

Nights I'd dream of it and days too –
of his mouth opening red as a furnace
and a laugh issuing, bright yellow.

That day. Black-haired Dad not hailing
neighbours, intent on the slag
beneath, turning it, picking
for coal with thick fingers.
Our fingers cold-clumsy picking too,
dropping dark nuggets into the sack,
quiet, saying nothing, watchful . . .
afraid of the hairs on his eyebrows,
the frost in his voice. "Po -lice!"
Two syllables hung on air . . . then
up, the pair of us in his iron hands,
chucked in the pram with the half-empty
sack and dour Dad bowling down the heap,
along the hawthorn lane, past the stream,
up Colonel's Walk and up Coburg Street,
the pram rattling and rollicking.

That day, eyes slammed, I heard Dad laugh.
The only time. That pure gold like the heart
of the fire. Terrifying.

Subjunctive

If I didn't know you
I could almost love you
the little boy blue sadness
in your eyes
the skill of your fingers
shaping wood

If I didn't know you
I could – almost – pity
your malt breath souring air
your fumbled fingers
that printed your children's
foreheads with lines
darkened their under-eyes to blue

But I know you well.
You're familiar as my own sad dog
eyes in the glass or that ugly
spatulate second finger
on my left hand, and because
I know you, my head is brimful
of an amber liquid that tastes of hate.
I gulp it till it makes me gag.

You

for my father, Martin Montgomery Wilkie

are dismembered dream-fragments –
a pocket sharp with nails,
a sole-stripped surreal boot
on a three-footed last,
an elusive blurry curve of eye
and bone, voice of a different cadence.
You are a jumbled jumble-sale jigsaw
I try to piece to waking
when, even when present,
you were always an absence.

You
are a half heard sad slow song
in a firelight room, an unseen
poker's scrape and grate at dawn,
a breadknife voice at a grainy table.
You are a symphony without an end
or beginning that I'd ghost-score,
notching the notes neat as nostrils
to a final rendering
when, even as I thought I had you,
you were always scattering.

You are a detail of landscape
glimpsed from a train, a certain
soaring field of flowering rape, a lake,
a configuration of tree and contour-line,
a sky streaked singular by a freak of sun.
You are that perfect place I promised
I'd return to view close-to, but that,
even on a map, I've never found my way back to.

A Day Almost Like Any Other

for my mother who died 24th April 1978

Last night I dreamed I was packing bones in brown paper.
I was fumble-fingered, the bones unwieldy,
the package clumsy as a fast-growing child.

I had to carry it from A to B to C and further,
stopping to retrieve dropped tibia and femur
to stuff them back in brown corrugations;
still by morning remembered the scrabble and scramble,
urgent time at my back fumbling clodhopper fingers
awkwarding cackhanded arms.

Trust me, Mother, I'll get you there whole
wherever there is   whatever whole means

Today I wrote of reflections – old woman, left child,
the mad boy – framed in windows – who returned
in the night to rattle my panes.

Don't knock, Mother,
just lift up the latch, walk in

Tonight I spent with women scanning lines on white paper,
sharing our tiny huge significance – a badger sighting,
the unsafety of havens, a letter unsent, a birth,
and improbably, a magical Mum. Truth is, I'd forgotten
till now, very late, that the date has its memory,
intrudes, won't be wrapped in brown paper and hidden
from view

you're the guest I'd forgotten was coming, but here
you're welcome   I'm opening every door and window now
for the bones to fly through   if it takes all night

I'll re-assemble you. If you'll just trust me, Mother,
I'll try to get you right this time   it's 2.12 am
twenty fifth of April 1989

and I can't see the fit of you for crying

PART TWO

LIVING WITH THEM

Almost

Have you ever watched a baby's eyes
watching yours – the way you drown
fathoms deep in each other's blue spaces
till there's just the one last dive
left to make before you disappear like air
into invisibility and every part of you
tingles with a sort of nervous ticking
that's both excitement and fear
and you wish there were something earthing
you – a ladder, rope, gantry, anything at all
though you don't entirely want to be earthed
either?

It's like transforming into your red cloth kite
at the seaside that the east wind caught and plumped
and tugged loose from the wooden crucifix
round which the string was figure-eighted and left
your hand empty, then dwindled smaller and smaller
to a tiny splat of red against the sky you had
to squint to see. Yes, it's almost like that.
Nearly.

Dust

8 a.m. I have wallpapered my daughters
in Laura Ashley today, light blue
thick-sprigged with small white
flowers. It suits their fair freshness
and my hankering mood for rootedness,
a slower time when women swished
as they strolled and snagged up burrs
and seedheads with their skirt frills.

My girls are pale rooms with windows open,
fresh linen on the beds and wildflowers –
forget-me-nots, maybe – in white china jugs.
They are rooms with time to sit, turn pages
and dream for a year – or maybe two – time
ordered precise as punctuation, commas, colons,
semis and fullstops making some sense of it all,
all of it driving at something.

All day I have snuffed up the air of these rooms
as though I hadn't created them, as though
they were made for me by someone else,
a mood's habitation that must be lived in
and through and over and over before the décor
needs changing, walls stripped bare and the panic
of choice and purchase, the choked moment
before the first cut strip, first brushstroke.

It's 5 p.m. I've baked scones and ladled amber jam
into a small glass bowl. In the blue vase
the last of the marigolds will die within the day.
My two girls open and slam doors. Flowers and blue
fall from their faces in streamers that I cup my hands
to catch and reinstate. Too late. Just nine hours –
time enough for someone to fingernail a join and rip
and rip, and now we're all dark mahogany, musty
drapes that muffle light and ugly leathery plants,
every leaf, every crease furry and fuzzed with dust.

Painting Carrie's Bedroom

A Mistake in Shade

I had thought to make her a leafy bower
full of cuckoo-call and calm to rest in,
to change shape as the sun moved,
trying on and casting off sunlight.

Dulux Matchmaker let me down,
or imagination that failed to foresee
these drowning depths of light-
absorbing green, rollers of shadow
that shipwreck the furniture
full fathom five, even in sun.

At these depths her pink curtains look blue, the
bedspread ripples like kelp,
her dreams, she says, are full of ocean,

and, having wanted cream or a pastel-green,
you blame me – can hardly speak for bile
as you dredge up other mistakes of mine.

I founder and drown in your green disapproval,
know it will take two coats or more
and years to make reparation.

Before The Hedge-Cutter Comes

for Lisa

You stand across the threshold
one foot in the doll's blank face to smash it
the other in the hormone flood;
extremities touch a past and a future
but for now you are eternal present
daughter of the cat's eyes slotted in just slant
daughter of the Rubens bum
daughter with breasts just blossoming
and elbows like arrows

just for now you are the rose at its peak
before the rain, dew, mildew, canker,
you are the moment before the phone-call
second before the head-turn
the three day glow of green before the spring

the gasp before tide going out
transforms to tide coming in
you are all that is brink and balance and brim
porch, verge, edge, rim

and for now safe, content in your brackets
of thorns and years. But under your
canted eyelids an old dream stirs.
In sleep your lips rehearse smiles
to welcome the man with the shears.

The Red Wellies

Entered the family fairy-tale as snugly
as Cinderella's glass slipper or the red-hot
shoes the Wicked Queen was made to dance in.

We've rehearsed so often your delight in them,
the way you kissed each one goodnight, cried when
it didn't rain the next day or the next.

Wet summer turned dry but I let you wear them –
cartoon L-shapes in brilliant postbox red
blip blapping as you swished through grass –

you'd need them, I knew if you were to ford puddles
dry-shod, then roads slick with wet, then shallow
streams to the further bank. I'd urge you, "Go on".

The first few times you looked over your shoulder,
your face painted with that strange mix of grin,
and grit that's so much yours even now,

my surly girl, who's too old for tales, rejects
remembering, all ready to swagger in your black Dee Ems
over seas and oceans without a single backward look.

Rehearsing Farewell

My first, most intransigent daughter
pushes the book over the space between us
her long fingers spread to hold pages
apart. "This is the one I'll choose
for the project. D'you like it?"

It is a bronze no larger than the stretch
of her thumb and first finger, rough cast
as if the two figures had burst the mould.
Even in one dimension the grief's as palpable
as the stuff of her blue jeans,   her skin.

Oh, the long arms of the child thrown round
the woman, face pressed into her mother's neck
you can almost hear the smothered cry
"Lass mich bleiben, Mutti." Mother,
don't send me away.

                                        And the woman?
One arm hangs limp at her side, the hand
scarcely clenched while the left lies
loose on the daughter's back, thumb
just grazing the hunch of the shoulder.

Those raised eyes and clamped mouth
might read anything – that maybe,
like me, she has no talent for suffering,
just numbs with pain like an animal.

I stare at the page where bronze strains
to split and print blurs. The black panes
of the window contain a tilted fragment
of the room we sit in, chairs and bookshelves
forlorn among branches of honeysuckle.

Her imminent leaving hurls me into that room
I only half recognise. My arms long
to throw themselves round her, my face
to press deep deep into her neck.

“Wonder what it’s called in German?” she asks,
then, seeing the tears, “For God’s sake, Mum,
d’you have to make everything so bloody dramatic?”

Living With Them

It's involuntary as sneezing
this compulsion to destroy
all we've so carefully erected
over twenty five years

convulsive as sternutation
their explosion through doors,
into rooms. We are condemned.
Atishoo, atishoo, we all fall down.

PART THREE

YOU TOO MAY SEE HARE

You Too May See Hare

In 1662 the Scottish witch, Isabel Gowdie, confessed that she had transformed herself into a hare by reciting the spell: "I shall go intill a hare, With sorrow and sych meickle care, And I shall go i' the De'il's name, Ay while I come home again." To change back into a woman, she repeated: "Hare, hare, God send thee care. I am in an hare's likeness now, But I shall be in a woman's likeness even now."

(i)

Hare Year

Leaf bare March
ice edged wind
grass winter thin
March was our rut

All of softening April
the shapes of you quickened
fisting the belly of me
April was my wait

till May – woods blued
with witches' thimbles
one cuckoo chimed contractions

Then my young straightway hopping
their full fur and wideopen eyes
their never-no-need of me
May was my completion

The rest is nothing –
ease of grain ripening
bough and ear heavy as vacancy
In August the silver sixpence bullet

I am small bone and dust
but the fisherman's creel is cursed
with the severed foot of me
I suck cows dry   Your dreams shudder
with my portendings

(ii)

At Skidmore's

The shop smells of dead blood.
The elder brother, reddish toupée awry,
has matt mad eyes. The younger lisps
among fifth rate fruit and veg, duck eggs
still shit- and feather-smeared.
A pet owl, alive still, glowers from topshelf gloom.
Here's a world seen through a glass clearly.
Only flowers could ever bring me –
profuse and cheap enough whatever season.
Today it's chrysanthemum bronze has hithered me
sideways-eyed past fowl and fur hanging
hamstrung from hooks. The old woman in front
wants hare – two hares. There's nowhere else
to stare as Skidmore unhooks, stuffs stiffened
flesh in plastic and exchanges coin . . . .
and at her turning my knees are buckled
by the thump of the lumpy leaden carrier.
I'm spinning in the rictus she makes, muttering
her shrill perfunctory   Sorry.

(iii)

Revisiting Michael

Hare-lip, cloven lip,
face warped into parody,
eyes dragged out of round
and tongue lost in the cleft.
Michael sans-words,
big ears antennaed for insult.

Remember: April wideawake morning
a snoring house and hare
click-creeping closer –
unlooked-for godsend.

Hare-lip, harebrain
jeered into madness,
quartering the playground
fumbling curses, wall-eyed fury
gone intill a hare
with sorrow and sych meickle care

Remember: a night's black bowl,
below arc lights' curve and a frieze
of grey dogs straining and the toy
on its wire crazily veering
gone i' the De'il's name

Harelip, split-lip,
learning, hard as flight,
to shape plosive, mould consonant,
force sound to word . . .   learning,
hard as fall, how word and fear
go hand in hand hame again

Remember Michael, edged closer
and closer, the leveret-heart of him
palpitating under my bone
something like panic,
something like love.

(iv)

Wildlife

Up on the moor above Tideswell
spring's a green aureole hint,
not a whisper of birdsong
through clenched windows.

My head is winter – bitter cold,
cram-packed with spite. My heart's
fisted like frost against them –
their pluckings at my sleeve,
their needs, always needs, shrinking
space small enough to a dot to swallow.

I'm up here to smoulder.
I'm up here to breathe.

Air's hollering at me – space acres
shouting me out. But every fibre's crimped,
fingers clipped to the still wheel.
The radio's talking wildlife, half-heard.

I try not to listen

                    . . . . I'm out here looking for hares. . . .

her triangular face, great gleamy eyes,
that sometime tremor and twitch of muscle
just below one ear

                    . . . . but unfortunately (windblown) there seem
                         to be no hares about today . . . .

his lying low when he scents approach
or reproach, his ears alert for invasion,
his big Jack swaggery hop-skippety-jump
braggadaccio air when we box words

The fury-cleaned glass is as clear as a retina
and look! The moor's freckle-spotted with hare
on hare intent on their crazy manoeuvres,
swervings, sudden armchair stops

. . . . It's such a pity. . . (a sad half-laugh)

and I'm laughing full from the belly,
turning the key, finding the gear,
accelerating back as mad as one

I shall be in a woman's likeness even now

PART FOUR

THIS AGE

Remember Orkney

where each day seemed like two
and milky light lingered till after eleven?

remember walking the dog in the still
and how the bullocks pushed so close to the fence

to watch, that the blunt fronts of their fore-
shortened heads were stamped with diamonds?

how they paralleled us, wistful and curious
till the wall cut them short, and we glanced back

to see them black and white bunched there
still staring after the golden dog?

We're miles and years further south now
each day's shorter than the one before

and I feel like one of those yearning beasts
penned in by stone and wire, unable to follow

where you're going, just able to peer after the blur
of your hair till distance swallows it and you.

These days I see the print of lines on my forehead
and some brute bit of me wants to bellow.

This Age

when each time you wake you find
something else is the matter with you

and doctor's appointments are regular
and frequent as Innovations Reports

where nouns both common or (more usually)
proper escape the mind like blenny eels

where every blessed thing – a cloud formation,
a fork, a geranium is an uncracked code;

where hours can be longer than a corpse's hair,
American male poems, a telephone bill

or speed past like Intercity expresses or
the whole of your personal history, drowning.

When some days you're high as an Iroquois
construction worker on a New York skyscraper

and sometimes more down than a drain, when
your body pulls you this way and that

like a dog on a lead in need of Obedience Classes,
when one minute you're a geyser, the next an ice-floe,

when veins start sprinting up your legs
like Russian vines and your waist's gone AWOL

and you really need bifocals or two pairs of specs
and your toenails are far more horny than you are.

Where sleep's like a line by Carol Ann Duffy
and you dream of a hole going right through the mattress

where you could stow your right arm till morning
when your ankles will cramp, knees crack, hands cack

or of ceilings and walls in need of plaster,
wallpaper unfurling like lime-green party poopers

when you talk to yourself like a lone budgerigar
on a ladder in a cage in front of a mirror

when your words repeat and repeat like indigestion
and you fear the men in white coming up the street

when you stare into space at the table
like the women in Last Year in Marienbad

where you realize the island you're wrecked on
is the result of a draughtsman's error

when you stand outside the window of yourself
scratching like Cathy to be let in, when

you smoke more, eat more, drink more, laugh less
when some days the only comfort is gravity –

the way the apple stays in the bowl,
the plaster remains on the ceiling.

Imitation

for Anna

We're laughing remembering Woollies when we
were teenagers in black and white before
they invented technicolour;   how everything
was imitation something else – long ropes
of pearls whose nacre you could flake off
with your nail, and mock silk scarves
(really rayon) and earrings of imitation jet.

Home was more of the same – new lino's random
grey veins, more marble than marble; posh wall
to wall carpet that stung like wasps but was good
as wool only twice as hard-wearing. Your Mum boasted
a teapot that was really a cottage – or vice-versa.
Mine was proud of five rigid artificial daffs
in a plaster vase in the window, facing out.

Even words were counterfeit – "a visit from your
Auntie", "a number two", "hanky-panky" and "passed
away" were cheap plastic versions of blood, shit,
sex and death that might shatter and cut.
We were force-fed the fake for so long it was hard
to recognise the real when we finally met it, harder
still to say we preferred it, then to prefer it.

Forty years on and in full colour we're counting
them over - our long ropes of synthetic pearls.
We're counting and naming them like bruises or grudges,
and though we're both laughing, there's a tin edge
to our laughter like that canned amplified stuff
that punctuates the jokes on TV comedy shows
that always makes you want to weep.

Another Visit to the Medium

Hopeful, I've come for the severalth time
to contact her. The wish is head-stored,
kept unsaid. She never spoke a lot to me
alive . . she does not now she's dead.

They've magicked me pragmatic Gran, burbling
about looking before I leap; they've hey-prestoed
Grandad who I hardly knew – He was a traveller,
was he? It's a beautiful view.

They've pulled Uncle George from the deep black hat,
a schoolfriend I hadn't known was dead. She warned
of a Marjorie. . . .or Maggie. . . . . . . .or Peg
She's weaving patterns around your head.

From a fathomless pocket they've whisked long-ago
cousins, an unrecognised child of seventeen
(Take it with you, my dear), Dad's brother, William,
great-aunts, neighbours etcetera. But as I feared

Mother hangs back. She'll not be flourished
by women   All touched in the head, or menopausal
most likely   They'll pluck her from no linings
like dove or scarf or never-ending hankie.

Yet she quite enjoyed pretence and illusion,
loved to tease with hints and winks and wait-
and-sees . . . . So long I've waited
and still not seen . . . . . . .Oh, Mother, please. .

I swear this is the last time.
I can't stand the after session blues.
Please, Ma, stop your hiding, do. Crash
through the æther, you awkward old bugger.
Come through.

Mata Kelap

No more than a speck – a tiny flake of soot
or cigarette-ash hovering nor-nor-west
of my left eye corner when I
swivel my head towards sun in the morning. . .

they call it a floater, entirely harmless
boding no ill at all but as mercury climbs
the column and the pointer swings to high
I know mata kelap is coming, my eye darkening. .

this is the age when it strikes, this cold
corridor between maturity and rot,
where things stand on their heads like acrobats
and vocabularies have all to be re-learned

where masks crumble to their components –
leather, feathers, cloth, clay – when most days
geese walk Chaplinesque over our graves
shuddering us in or out of sun . . . .

neither you nor I will know till it's here
no warning's given, just the glitter of steel
in sunlight, incoherent cries, carnations
of arterial blood in gutters on the street

such a good wife, mother, neighbour, friend, they'll say,
till her eye darkened. For those who didn't know me at
all, reading that such a monster walked unnoticed
and unremarkable among them every day, will appal.

mata kelap – "the dark eye" – a Javanese term for the phenomenon of running amok.

Miep's Gift

(after the television play "The Attic" which recounted the life of Miep, the Dutchwoman who helped the Frank family in hiding from the Nazis.)

I.m. Ann Frank. And all the others.

Red shoes with heels
fit for dancing
if there had been space
for dancing
in the attic's hugger-mugger
the world's constriction.

Red heeled shoes
fit for strolling
if there had been pavements
left unspattered by hate
fewer yellow stars to illumine
the curfew's dark.

Red shoes, suede and secondhand,
eminently fit for a girl
turned almost woman
if there had been time for turning.

Red suede secondhand shoes
with cuban heels
escaped through time and space
from the hugger-mugger of piles
and piles and piles
of multi-coloured empty shoes
to dance on our screens
to footprint our complacencies.

Gretel Speaks

How I looked up to you! Beneath the dirndl
my knees sweated with admiration.
Big brother, mind on fire with plans and schemes,
a genius at Maths, a whizz at crosswords,
thinking straight as a pine, while mine . . .
"Look at Hansel," Father said when, dreaming,
I dropped and tripped and burned. "Emulate Hansel!"
I watched. I tried to emulate.
Some soft quick of me turned to rock;
I learned to think against the moon,
to speak abstraction, to classify and name.
I stopped flying with the swallows.

How I was glad of you when the time came,
whispering your foiling plans in the dark and,
when the downstairs talk-buzz ceased, going unafraid
out into night to gather pebbles. O your rooster laugh,
my brave, clever brother! I melted in the conspiracy
of your wink – dared not ask, daredn't even think
And if there is no moon? And that other time. . .
How I envied your purpose, bating of present pleasure
to net a future. My mouth gagged for bread.
Juices made my mouth a fire. I feared mockery too much
to question, If there are birds there?

Then later, I pitied you, weeping your spleen
in the cage, the brain's convolutions cracking apart
with plots, your fingers' plumpness. And your eyes
blind as stones to seduction – the hot exciting kitchen,
the slatternly woman telling me new tales, sweet
to my tongue as barley-sugar. Tight within rock
things stirred and moved. Poor little brother,
closer than father or mother or husband, I cried
for our closeness, for the blood curled thick as rope
between us. I love you, mein Bruderchen,
as we lick your bones clean, burn your skin and hair
in the fire, weave dreams in your smoke.

She and I speak of mysteries you would have explained.
I never dared say I preferred the first to the latter.
It wasn't moon or swifts misled you. Where you are now,
can you forgive me, Hansel? Or does none of it matter?

Sally's House

White, neurasthenic as crocus
or their house's blind lace windows
that mirrored all, saw nothing,
Sally shrinks from us.

Like their Staffordshire pottery dogs
guarding the mantel that failed
to bark at stair-creaking intruder
or a child's cry, Sally will not speak
(though she screamed at the leaving
Let me stay! promising to be good.)

We wave wands to expand nipped gestures
into daisy-chains of bright silk scarves,
to explode muteness into fanfares
of extravagant crepe flowers.
But magic demands accomplice,
not accuser. Sally's silences accuse

Daily, despairing, we have practised our art
and daily her Star of Bethlehem eyes
see through our sleight of hand – she knows
too well the treachery of palm and finger;
discoveries of gold coins in her ears
are metaphors only for other invasions.

Nor do the simpler tricks succeed;
she too has learned concealment and
wiser than we she mistrusts illusion,
awaits the fortuitous miracle – the sixth dove
emerging when hands had hid only five.

Today Sally, silently, proffers her picture –
silent house faint in pink pencil,
three uncurtained windows, a tiny trapezoid door,
one isosceles chimney, one smoke signal spiral

and, past masters at deception, we
are crucified on the purple kisses
that cram all the space on the page
her own house does not fill.

Reluctant Samaritan

Just my luck. Always the same –
sitting good as gold on a bus
or train, minding my business
and a dozen empty seats but guess
who plonks down in the one next to mine?
Every time! Today she's wearing one
man's boot and a slipper, lipstick
smeared to an ear, an outrageous yellow
hat. "He was a get, that bloody Churchill.
Aren't onions a price? D'you like my hat?
I hate him – that twat over there."

How glare? How swerve my eyes and window-
stare when her red raw fingers turn and turn
the ten pee piece, when her words grope
in my head, when there but for the grace of. . . . .?
Her stop will always be mine –
if I went to the end of the Line
she'd be going there too.

I blame you, Mother – that half-smile
always hovering, that peeled gaze that fetched
gypsies, tramps, lost dogs and hurt kids
to litter our rooms like leaves while you
dispensed sympathy and tea and T.C.P.
like there was no tomorrow. And then bequeathed
me them – eyes too wide-open, ears pitched
for sorrow, a freak turn of mouth beckoning

till of course they come – the unloved, unlovely,
the unloveable; the confused, those in whom
the pattern's scotched; those who'll take a mile
for the proffered inch. The books say
it's our deprived childhood – in succouring others
we care for our selves. I'm not sure deprived's
the right word. Oh, Lord, look where it comes,
wambling lopsidedly in my direction. Straight into
my collection. Another crippled duck. Just my luck!'

Journey
for Llyn Wilson

This one I'm on that I'd no wish,
only a need to take, is uncomfortable,
sordid even, seated in the train's
arse-end with other smokers and misfits,
oddities and their slightly scruffy kids,
and the air-conditioning not working
and getting to the Buffet car situated,
according to the conductor speaking,
towards the front of the train and
now open, scarcely worth the hassle;
this journey I'd renegue on if I could
is bloody lonely and the tunnels scarey
and dark and my face in the window's very
pale and hardly like me at all, and
when another Intercity going in the opposite
direction screams past it's like a knife
that's just missed its target; and the other
end of the compartment there's a bloke
who's the spit of my dead Dad and no way
do I want to talk to him, and then he starts
talking into a mobile phone and I realize
my memory's deceived me and I don't know
why I should care so much or so little,
why I should care; and this book's not at all
interesting and the style's bleeding terrible
and the landscape, though lovely,'s outside
and untouchable, and there's the other end
to get to and get through, to where? to what?
and what for?
I'm onto my fourth cigarette and planning
to broach the staggering Buffet approach
for a couple of cans of overpriced lager
and a hot bacon and tomato burger when
you materialise in the seat next to mine
and say, "What you need's a companion.
I'll be it, if you like?" And I say,

“I would like that. Thanks.” and your eyebrows lilt slightly mockingly the way they do, and you grab hold of my hand when the train rattles over the points and the rain starts.

Problems of Translation

I'm trying to follow the printed instructions
to assemble this appliance and not managing –
it's in my language – I recognise every word
yet some strange shuffling of syntax and grammar
has ruined sense. It might as well be Japanese

and I have to smile remembering you at six
up to your eyebrows in sand creating castles
along with a gang of French kids, garrulous
then as you are now in your need to share
every act, every thought or fancy in words,

how you spoke English to them with perfect
French inflections and gestures that mirrored
theirs so that they answered you in French, though
puzzlement crinkled their sunburnt foreheads
as they bent again to their moats and forts.

Mountain

Once we were one mountain,

our volumes and contours one.
We stood as one in the weather.

When cloud-shadow played,
we couldn't say it painted
your side or mine. All sides were ours.

There were tremors and tremblings,
subterranean murmurings all along.
We were smug, though, refusing to name them

till that day when sub-surface things
collided. The crash and the crust that held us
cracked wide open . . . . . that day.

We are both smaller now.
A black river snakes between
your dark foothills and mine,

and there is no boatman to carry us
each to each other's cleaving.
We are still learning both, each, other.

Today things are moving
in the black river-water's coils,
new things, pallid and nameless, rise,

trying to find some purchase
on mud and rock, then haltingly
crawling upward – some on your side, some on mine.

A Proper Goodbye

Another Easter gone like every
godforsaken Easter since the one
she abandoned me. Years of the world's
indifference – lent-lilies pushing up
and open, birdsong, trees leafing,
lambs drifting fields like pocks of snow –
it's only now I know how futile is
this loving of the dead, how hollow
the left child's howl has become.
I always did find it hard to say
Farewell, Goodbye, I who always cry
at partings however temporary,
but the time's come. I have to
turn with a whole heart to what
is left to me – the living –
and love them.

JACQUELINE BROWN was born in Pontefract, West Yorkshire in 1944, and was educated there and at the University of Newcastle-upon-Tyne, where she gained a B.A. in French and English. It was a course run by the poet U.A. Fanthorpe at the Arvon Foundation that started her off on her own writing career, although it is only now, some ten years later, that she feels able to describe herself as a poet.

Her work has appeared in a wide variety of magazines and journals including *The Observer*, *Poetry Review* and *Staple*, and her first collection of poems, *Accidental Reality* was published by Littlewood in 1989. In 1992, she had the distinction of winning the first prize in the Observer/Arvon Poetry Competition with the then unpublished sequence of poems *Thinking Egg* (Arc Publications 1993). She has received Yorkshire and East Midlands Arts Bursaries, an Arts Council Award and a Hawthornden Fellowship.

Having taught for many years both in this country and abroad, Jacqueline Brown currently teaches creative writing at the W.E.A. and also to people with mental health problems. She lives with her husband and two daughters in Derbyshire.